William Stubbs

The Medieval Kingdoms of Cyprus and Armenia

Two lectures delivered Oct. 26 and 29, 1878

William Stubbs

The Medieval Kingdoms of Cyprus and Armenia
Two lectures delivered Oct. 26 and 29, 1878

ISBN/EAN: 9783337245610

Printed in Europe, USA, Canada, Australia, Japan

Cover: Foto ©ninafisch / pixelio.de

More available books at **www.hansebooks.com**

ARMENIA.

Two Lectures delivered Oct. 26 and 29, 1878, by WILLIAM STUBBS, M.A., Regius Professor of Modern History, Fellow of Oriel College, Honorary Student of Christ Church, and Honorary Fellow of Balliol College; Rector of Cholderton.

[These lectures make no claim to the character of original research. They are simply notes on the more noteworthy parts of a subject which has long had a great interest for the writer, and which for the moment may catch the attention of intelligent students.

The labours of French scholars in this field have been so thorough and exhaustive, that, except in the monuments which may exist on the soil of Cyprus and Armenia, little room is left for discovery.]

CONTENTS.

THE MEDIEVAL KINGDOMS OF CYPRUS AND ARMENIA.

I HOPE that I need not apologise for my choice of a subject. The events of the last two years can scarcely be called to mind without much misgiving, both as to the way in which they have been construed by contemporary readers, and as to the way in which they will be judged by history. I am not one of those who hold that the maintenance of an opinion contrary to their own belief, implies either moral delinquency or mental imbecility. I have been quite prepared to admit that two honest men, equally gifted and alike trying to be impartial, may come to diametrically opposite conclusions from the same evidence. But it is sickening to see the policy of a statesman, still more to see the question of a fact, debated, maintained or contradicted, by advocates whose arguments are not based upon attempts to find out the truth, but are simply weapons of attack and defence. "This is to be believed because it suits the party; this is to be discredited because it would damage the party: this is true because Pericles has said it; this is false, or why should Alcibiades, or Cleon, or whoever it may be, have called heaven and earth to witness that it is true?" It will be a good thing, if, after so much that is disheartening in the popular treatment of great questions, even one little benefit may be secured. Whatever may be thought of the Anglo-Turkish convention, on whatever grounds, moral or political, we may determine that the salvation of Turkey is possible, or that Cyprus is an unhealthy island,

B

a professor of History may draw some little comfort from the fact that the attention of people has been called to a portion of the history of Christendom of which little notice has been taken of late years, and which is closely connected with one of the greatest movements that ever affected the history of the world. Having said this I will add, that my object in this lecture is not to ventilate dogmas, to impress any principle moral or political, or to justify any foregone conclusion. I plead guilty to the charge brought against me of choosing subjects which are of no importance to any human being; I wish simply to talk about a subject on which a good deal of intelligent interest has arisen, and in the further discussion of which many fresh points of interest may be expected to present themselves.

It is right however that I should preface one word of caution against myself. The Crusades are not, in my mind, either the popular delusions that our cheap literature has determined them to be, nor papal conspiracies against kings and peoples, as they appear to the Protestant controversialist; nor the savage outbreaks of expiring barbarism thirsting for blood and plunder, nor volcanic explosions of religious intolerance. I believe them to have been, in their deep sources, and in the minds of their best champions, and in the main tendency of their results, capable of ample justification. They were the first great effort of medieval life to go beyond the pursuit of selfish and isolated ambitions; they were the trial-feat of the young world, essaying to use, to the glory of God and the benefit of man, the arms of its new knighthood. That they failed in their direct object is only what may be alleged against almost every great design which the great disposer of events has moulded to help the world's progress; for the world has grown wise by the experience of failure, rather than by the winning of high aims. That the good they did was largely leavened with evil may be said of every war that has ever been waged; that bad men rose by them

while good men fell, is and must be true wherever and whenever the race is to the swift and the battle to the strong.
But that in the end they were a benefit to the world no one
who reads can doubt; and that in their course they brought
out a love for all that is heroic in human nature, the love of
freedom, the honour of prowess, sympathy with sorrow, per-
severance to the last, and patient endurance without hope, the
chronicles of the age abundantly prove; proving moreover
that it was by the experience of those times that the forms
of those virtues were realised and presented to posterity.
This much I say, by way of a caution, that you may not accuse
me of an attempt to impose upon you. The history of the
Crusades has always had for me an interest that quite rivals
all the interest I could take in the history of the Greeks and
Romans; and very much of that interest is of the same sort;
a half archæological interest in a life and growth from which
we have ourselves received some great impulses, but almost
all the minutiæ of which are important only through their connexion with those great impulses. Such a half archæological
interest I hope you may feel in the history of medieval Cyprus,
and what little is to be told of its sister kingdom.

The last decade of the twelfth century saw the establish-
ment of two small Christian kingdoms in the Levant, which
long outlived all other relics of the Crusades except the military
orders; and which, with very little help from the West, sustained
a hazardous existence in complete contrast with almost every-
thing around them. The kingdoms of Cyprus and Armenia
have a history very closely intertwined, but their origin and
most of their circumstances were very different.

By Armenia as a kingdom, is meant little more than the ancient
Cilicia, the land between Taurus and the sea, from the frontier of
the principality of Antioch, eastward, to Kelenderis or Palæo-
polis, a little beyond Seleucia; this territory, which was com-
puted to contain sixteen days' journey in length, measured
from four miles of Antioch, by two in breadth, was separated

[4]

from the Greater Armenia, which before the period on which
we are employed had fallen under the sway of the Seljuks,
by the ridges of Taurus[1]. The population was composed
largely of the sweepings of Asia Minor, Christian tribes which
had taken refuge in the mountains. Their religion was partly
Greek, partly Armenian, for the Armenian Catholicos, after
resting for a century and a half in Mesopotamia, took refuge
at Sis, and founded there an independent or national Catholicate
at the close of the thirteenth[2] century. Their rulers were
princes descended from the house of the Bagratidæ, who had
governed the Greater Armenia as kings from the year 885
to the reign of Constantine Monomachus, and had then merged
their hazardous independence in the mass of the Greek empire[3].
After the seizure of Asia Minor by the Seljuks, the few of
the Bagratidæ who had retained possession of the mountain
fastnesses of Cilicia or the strongholds of Mesopotamia, acted
as independent lords, showing little respect for Byzantium save

---

[1] The boundaries of Armenia at its greatest extension are thus given by Du Laurier,
in the Armenian volume of the Recueil des Historiens des Croisades, pp. xix, sq. :—
Westward, Side or Eski-Adalieh ; eastward, the Pylæ Ciliciæ, or passes of the mountains close to the gulf of Alexandretta. The custom-house, towards Iconium, was at
Pilerga, and the passes Westward were at Germanicopolis and Claudiopolis.
[2] The Catholicate was without fixed residence from 1066–1114 ; it was then settled
at Hrom-Gla, on the Euphrates, in the principality of Edessa, where it remained until
1292, when it settled at Sis.
[3] The Armenian historians describe the Greater Armenia after the fall of the Arsa-
cidæ, under Arsaces IV, A.D. 387, as divided between Persia and Byzantium ; the
Arsacide rulers governing as tributaries until 428. From 428 to 625, it was governed
by Persian governors, " Marzbans," frequently native Armenians of the house of the
Bagratidæ ; from 632 by a Curopalates or patrician named at Constantinople ; sometimes by the patriarch, sometimes by the Khalif. In 885 the Bagratide, Aschod I,
was recognised by the Khalif Motamed as king, and was crowned. His successors
were Sempad I, 890 ; Aschod II, 914 ; Apas, 928 ; Aschod III, the Merciful, 952
Sempad II, 977 ; Kakig I, 989 ; John Sempad and Aschod IV, 1020 ; Interregnum,
1040 ; Kakig II, 1042. Kakig gave up his kingdom to Constantine Monomachus in
1045, and was murdered in 1079. These kings reigned at Ani. There was another
principality at Kars, which surrendered to Constantine Ducas in 1064. Senekerim
John, king of Vasburagan, had, in 1021, surrendered to Basil II, and received Sebaste
in Cappadocia ; and Abelgarib had Tarsus as a separate lordship from Constantine
Monomachus in 1042.—The Bagratidæ claimed an Israelite origin. St. Martin,
Mémoires Historiques et Géographiques sur l'Arménie.

where there was something to be gained. Such was the lord Taphnuz of Edessa, on whose inheritance Baldwin of Boulogne founded his principality; such were the lords Leo, Thoros, Melier and Rupin of the Mountains, who ruled Cilicia during the twelfth century; trying to balance their position between the Byzantine and Latin influences on each side of them. Rupin of the Mountain was prince at the time of the capture of Jerusalem by Saladin; he died in 1189, and his successor, Leo or Livon, after having successfully courted the favour of pope and emperor, was recognised as king of Armenia by the emperor Henry VI, and crowned by Conrad of Wittelsbach, archbishop of Mainz, in 1198. This act which, although Livon fortified his position by obtaining recognition from Alexius Angelus, implied a cessation of the old dependence on Byzantium, and an ecclesiastical reconciliation with Rome, was the typical act of Armenian history; the whole of which, save and except the defence against the Saracens and the Tartars of a later date, was an attempt to secure independence by skilful balancing of Greek and Roman influences; to obtain money from the West and arms from Constantinople, to obtain alternate alliances by royal marriages, and ecclesiastical freedom by regular variations between the two poles. For this latter policy the position of the Armenian Church was peculiarly fitted. It was so far schismatic as not to be integrally a portion of either Roman or Byzantine obedience, and so little heretical that its alliance was courted by both communions. Hence its importance in the conciliar history of the middle ages; an importance which has no sufficient parallel in the secular history of Armenia.

The origin of the Latin kingdom of Cyprus is less obscure and more romantic. Cyprus had been seized by the Arabs in the early days of Islam (cir. 700–cir. 963), but recovered for the empire by Nicephorus Phocas, and ruled by dukes down to the reign of Manuel Comnenus. Its population was a mixed one; there were Griffons or Greeks, Armenians, Georgians, Maronites, native Cypriots, Greek parœci, emancipated slaves, the descendants of

Albanian soldiery of the empire, and of Venetian emigrants
of the first Crusade. But the land was fertile, and they had
dwelt together in peace. In the reign of Manuel the happy days
of Cyprus ended and the period of calamity began. According to
the anchorite Neophytus, who wrote the tract "de Calamitatibus
Cypri," the native authority for the conquest by Richard Cœur
de Lion, Isaac Comnenus, a nephew of the emperor Manuel,
had been appointed by him to rule the Armenian frontier ; he
had quarrelled with the Armenians, been taken prisoner and
sold to the Latins ; that is, to Bohemond III of Antioch, whose
step-father, Reginald of Châtillon, had many years before ravaged
the isle of Cyprus in revenge for the hostility of Manuel Comnenus. He was ransomed from captivity by the emperor
Andronicus, and, about the year 1184, came to Cyprus and set
up an independent tyranny. He called himself βασιλεὺς, but
ruled as a despot of the worst order. All the better class
of Greek inhabitants fled to Constantinople ; and the state of
Cyprus under Isaac Comnenus was only paralleled by that of
Jerusalem under Saladin. On the evidence of Neophytus,
Richard of England came not as a freebooter, but as a deliverer
from utter misery. In this point there is a fair consensus of
Eastern and Western testimony. Richard seized Cyprus not as
a pirate, but as an avenger and emancipator. The story is short,
or may be made so.

After wintering at Messina, Richard having with him, in his
fleet, not in his ship, his betrothed wife Berengaria and his sister,
queen Johanna of Sicily, sailed for Acre on the 10th of April,
1191 ; the fleet was dispersed by a storm on Good Friday,
April 12 ; and Richard, after being obliged to land at Rhodes,
was driven by a second storm on the 1st of May into the Gulf
of Satalia. Before this day the queens had appeared off Cyprus,
and found anchorage off Limasol. Isaac had attempted by
courteous offers to get them into his power, but his hospitality
was presented in so military a fashion, that the guardians of the
royal ladies took fright, and avoided landing. On the very day

on which they were obliged to promise that they would go on
shore, Richard's ship came in sight. His first act was to demand
from Isaac an account of the treatment of the wrecked vessels
which had been driven on the coast of the island and plundered
by the emperor. Isaac replied contumeliously, and Richard
landed in force. On the 6th of May Limasol was taken : the
emperor was unhorsed by Richard in single combat, and fled to
Nicosia. On the 12th of May Richard and Berengaria were
married at Limasol ; and Berengaria was there crowned, not
queen of Cyprus, for the island was not yet taken or claimed,
but queen of the English. Negotiations for peace and alliance
were on foot, when Isaac suddenly broke off the deliberations and
fled to Famagosta. Richard, who had now obtained the assistance of Guy of Lusignan and the prince of Antioch, and who was
much pressed for time, left him no rest. Guy employed himself in
capturing the chief strongholds ; Richard, who was ill, after taking
Buffevento, occupied Nicosia. There the emperor submitted to
him on the 31st of May, and surrendered himself, his daughter
and his treasures. Richard put him in silver chains, having promised that he would not put him in irons ; placed the little girl
under charge of the queen, and spent or distributed his treasure.
Cyprus was conquered in a fortnight. Richard bestowed on the
island the inestimable gift of his presence for five days after the
emperor surrendered : Isaac he sent off under the charge of
Ralph Fitz-Godfrey to Tripoli ; he extorted from the Cypriots
half their property, in return for a charter by which the laws
of Manuel Comnenus were restored to them ; constables were
placed in the several castles, and Richard Camville and Robert
of Turnham were left behind to govern Cyprus as justices and
sheriffs on the English model [1]. What followed is not very clear.
Before a month was over Camville was dead, and Turnham had
been obliged to put down a revolt and hang a pretender. Richard
found his new acquisition a burden ; Neophytus briefly says that

---

[1] Ric. Divis. c. 61.

the " Incliter" sold the island for 200,000 pounds of gold to the
Latins. The Templars were the purchasers ; they also found the
burden a heavy one, especially at a moment when the war with
Saladin demanded all their energies. The small garrison which
they were able to keep in the island was shut up in Nicosia by
the angry Griffons, and there was every chance that Cyprus
would be lost as rapidly as it had been won. This was the state
of affairs in May 1192, when Richard, by a piece of rough diplomacy, prevailed on Guy of Lusignan to surrender his claim to
the shadowy crown of Jerusalem, and to accept the lordship of
Cyprus instead. The Templars were glad enough to sell their
rights, and Guy, with Richard's advice, bought them. A successful sally of the garrison of Nicosia saved the Latins from
massacre, the alarm of which they avenged by an indiscriminate
slaughter of the Greeks. Guy thus obtained his first hold on
the island ; so much of the Greek population as was still spared
fled in panic ; and way was thus made for the institution, in this
remote corner of the Levant, of a dynasty and government
of the straitest feudal character; the introduction into a land,
empty of all but the cultivating classes and slaves, of the fully
developed and now crystallised block of feudal polity.

The house of Lusignan maintained itself in Cyprus for nearly
three centuries, during which, although fallen somewhat from
the blessedness which had been broken up by Isaac Comnenus,
the island seems to have retained so much fertility and prosperity
internally as to make its later history very dark by contrast.
The flight of the Greek population, which had begun under
Isaac and been completed after the massacre of Nicosia, left the
island open to colonists from the West. The peculiar privileges
of the Cypriot Church, which was autocephalous, made it easy
for the remaining prelates and people to accept the Western
obedience, and enabled the house of Lusignan to appeal confi-
dently for the support of European Christendom. The short
period too during which, under Guy and his successor, the
administration of Cyprus was kept separate from that of the

waning kingdom of Palestine, gave those kings a moment's breathing time, and this they improved with a success which the long continuance of their dynasty against fearful odds may be held to prove.

Guy, we are told, received Cyprus for life only, and did homage for the island to Richard. As he already bore the title of king, the question whether he should hold Cyprus as a kingdom does not seem to have arisen. He appears in the Lignages d'Outremer as 'seignor,' not as 'roi de Chypre;' and no coins occur on which he is called king of Cyprus. On his death, in April 1194, Richard putting in no claim for the reversion, his brother, Amalric of Lusignan, constable of Palestine, entered on the possession as his heir; he was not as yet King of Jerusalem; it was a matter of importance to him to be recognised as King of Cyprus; and he accordingly did homage to the Emperor Henry VI. He was crowned by the Bishop of Hildesheim, who was sent over from Sicily to perform the ceremony; this was done in 1197. Immediately after this, Amalric succeeded to the crown of Jerusalem; the crown of Jerusalem which, after the year 1269, became permanently united with that of Cyprus, was an independent crown, and the king of Jerusalem an anointed king: the union of the crowns therefore seems to have precluded any question as to the tenure by which the kingdom of Cyprus should be held. The crown of Cyprus was conferred at Nicosia, that of Jerusalem at Tyre or at Acre, and, after the capture of Acre, at Famagosta. The homage then due to Richard or to the crown of England ceased at the death of Guy; although the discontented barons of Cyprus are said to have revived the idea of such a relation when they wanted the aid of Edward I, in 1271. The homage secured to the Emperor by Amalric was possibly recognised until 1269, but was throughout complicated by the claims of Frederick II and his sons on the kingdom of Jerusalem. In 1459 the illegitimate pretender, James II, did homage to the Sultan of Egypt as suzerain of Cyprus; but that act was not the recognition of a right; it was only a bid for support, and was one of the immediate causes of the entire downfall of the house of Lusignan. Guy, however, does not seem to have troubled himself about his title. His reign lasted only two years, and his whole time was given to the restoration of something like prosperity in the desolate land [1]. According to the contemporary ' Chronique d'Outremer' he opened an asylum for the dispossessed Franks of Armenia and Palestine. These, to the amount of 300 knights and 200 men-at-arms, with a great number of bourgeois, he enfeoffed with estates of land in Cyprus; so liberal was he that he retained for himself only twenty knights' fees. Possibly the truth was that he was obliged to sell the land of the island to find the money due to the Templars; but the mode in which it was done proves that the feudal idea, on which a few years later the Latin conquests in Romania were apportioned, was full grown. The arrangement however made by Guy had to be altered by Amalric when he reached the dignity of kingship. He threw himself on the mercy of his vassals; they responded liberally, and surrendered to him so many of his brother's grants that at his death a royal revenue of 200,000 byzants was forthcoming. Guy had perhaps made as much as he cared to make of his life interest, but he was, like his patron, careless in the spending of money, whilst unlike Richard's, his opportunities of acquiring it were very limited.

Thus, however, the land system of Cyprus was restored; the 300 knights, 200 men-at-arms, and extensive bourgeoisie constituted one or two permanent estates of the kingdom. The nobles, who were, no doubt, included in the number of the knights, were the numerous lords who had either fled before

---

[1] There were five classes of native cultivators in Guy's time :—
    (1) Parici—πάροικοι—slave cultivators.
    (2) Lefteri—ἐλεύθεροι—freed folk.
    (3) Albanesi—descendants of Albanian soldiery.
    (4) Veneziani bianchi—descended from the soldiers of Vital Michaele in the first Crusade.
    (5) Perperiarii enfranchised Paroeci—paying a tax of 15 perperi ; (cited from Bustron by Beugnot, Assizes of Jerusalem, i. 207).

Saladin, or were so little hopeful of the event of the Crusades, that they thought it wise to look to Cyprus as a prospective refuge. Hence throughout the middle ages the Cypriot lords retained the titles of their homes in Palestine ; and the Palestine titles, when the families of their possessors were extinct, were conferred as a sort of life peerage at the will of the kings. Of the few Frank families that showed any vitality the house of Ibelin was far the most prominent and prolific ; the lords of Ibelin and Mirabel, sprung from the house of Puiset, viscounts of Chartres, and closely connected with the counts of Champagne and Blois[1], had played a conspicuous part during the twelfth century in Palestine ; they were still more prominent in Cyprus : from them the royal house received wives and guardians for the infant kings ; two of the great recorders of the Assizes of Jerusalem were lords of Ibelin ; one as regent or bailiff of Cyprus conducted the valiant resistance to the claims of Frederick II : and in fact, if any one had cared to write it, the fortunes of the house of Ibelin would have been as great part of the history of Cyprus as those of the house of Lusignan. Other great families were those of Gibeleth and Bethsan, named from Byblus and Bethshan or Scythopolis. The whole peerage of Cyprus however contained only a few names, which sound strangely enough, as they illustrate the geographical unity of history. There were princes of Antioch, Galilee, and Montreal, lords of Beyrout, Sidon, Toron, Cæsarea, Tyre, and Tiberias, counts of Jaffa, Tripoli, and Carpasso ; there were also, as grand serjeanties, the double stewardships, constableships, and marshalships of Cyprus and Jerusalem and the chamberlainship of Cyprus ; these are all or

---

[1] Balian le François, the first of the family, is described in the Lignages d'Outremer as brother of count Guillin de Chartres ; by which we are to understand that he was a relation of Hugh de Puiset, count of Joppa, son of Everard, and grandson of Geldewin, viscount of Chartres. His name Balian is probably a softened form of Waleran ; see Du Cange on the Lignages, pp. 360, 361. One lady of this house married an English knight, Hamo l'Estrange, who died in Palestine about 1272 ; this was Isabella, daughter of the lord of Berytus and widow of the young king, Hugh III. See Assizes of Jerusalem, ii. 449.

nearly all. They constituted a high court of baronage or parliament, as they had done in Palestine, and were the supreme council of the king, of which we have so much information in the Assizes of Jerusalem.

As for the ecclesiastical estate, tradition assigns also to King Guy some trenchant measures which help to complete the parallel or the contrast between him and William the Conqueror. The old Cypriot church had an archbishop and fourteen suffragans; the archbishop was archbishop of Cyprus, and owed obedience to no patriarch. The flight or submission of the Greeks left the field open to the Latin clergy; and Guy placed a Latin archbishop at Nicosia, with suffragans at Famagosta, Limasol and Baffo. This arrangement was sanctioned by Celestine III, in 1196. As time went on, the Greek clergy returned and Jacobites and Nestorians followed; very uneasy relations were produced between the two chief hierarchies, one of which depended on Rome, whilst the other, now seated at Famagosta, claimed the ancient prerogative of the Cypriot church. The schismatic clergy were however subjected by Honorius III to the Latin bishops, whilst Alexander IV, in the year 1260, went so far as to forbid the election of a Greek archbishop after the death of the reigning prelate, and reduced the number of Greek sees to four, Soli, Leucara, Arsinoe, and Carpasso; the bishops were also subjected to the Latin metropolitan, who was bound to administer justice among them. Probably Guy has obtained credit for some of the measures which properly belong to the popes and to a later date. The clergy of the island were as numerous as the difference of nationalities required. The Mendicant orders formed the strength of the Latin portion, the secular priests that of the Greek and Armenian. Monasteries abounded. In Nicosia alone were 250 churches. These then being the estates of the realm, the powerful people were all Franks, the returning Greeks and Armenians would only creep into an equality of privilege, or return into the enjoyment of their old customs, as the governing race allowed; and, although they ultimately grew and prevailed

while the governing race dwindled and perished, all political
interest centres in the governing race. For them the existing
polity of Palestine was transported across the sea ; not as yet
reduced to writing, for the system of Godfrey of Bouillon, the
Letters of the Sepulchre, if it were ever codified, had perished,
and the Assizes had not yet taken their historic form. But the
new kingdom was singularly rich in lawyers, and this was early
recognised ; in 1214 we find Lewis of France, son of Philip II,
applying for a legal opinion on a point of procedure to Hugh I
of Cyprus ; the old lords of Palestine spent their leisure in Cyprus
recording the customs of their lost inheritance, and the extant
Assizes of Jerusalem were the result of their studies. The
names of the great legists are Philip of Navarre, John and
James of Ibelin, and Guy le Tort. John of Ibelin, who died in
1266, and bore the title of count of Jaffa, Ramlah (Rames), and
Ascalon, drew up the existing Assize of the High Court. It is
in exact symmetry with Western usage, that this great compila-
tion was not received as a code until the year 1369 : like the
" Siete Partidas " of Alfonso the Wise, it was but a body of
jurisprudence, the use of which depended on its own reasonable-
ness, or a collection of customs which were recorded because
they were used, not merely used because they were recorded.
The Highest Law was still " the custom " recorded in the heart
and mouth of the " lawful man."

The Assizes of Jerusalem, then, although no doubt they describe
what we may call the common law of the Cypriot kingdom, so far
as concerned the Franks, cannot be regarded during the greater
part of the period as an authoritative code ; the native population
of Cyprus, like the native Syrians of Palestine, had laws and
customs, such perhaps as the laws of Manuel Comnenus, for
which they obtained Richard's confirmation ; and the city of Famagosta at a little later period, after having been for some years under
the government of the Genoese, was allowed to retain the laws of
Genoa. Within the feudal fabric itself, custom or perhaps principle was more dominant than law ; the lords of the great fiefs

did not accept the rules of the high court as binding unless they
had themselves consented to them ; the unity of feudal jurisprudence lay rather in ideas than in cogent uniformity. Add to
this the fact that the Frank population of Cyprus showed no
tendency to ordinary increase, but was either constantly dimin-
ishing or recruited by arrivals from the West, whilst the Greek
population was at home, strong, numerous and wealthy; that
the Latin Church accordingly, although powerful in the protec-
tion of Rome and of the Cypriot crown, was surpassed in wealth
and historical greatness by the Greek and Armenian communities ;
and we cannot but conclude that in this, which is regarded as the
most flourishing period of Cypriot history, there was little chance
of strong government or administrative development. The
Assizes of Jerusalem lay like a crystal block, a model of usages,
incapable of enforcement and incapable of growth. The kings
lived for the most part the life of adventurers or knights-errant,
playing their part in the defence of Christendom, but still, like
the great military orders and fragmentary principalities of Palestine, only as an isolated garrison in the middle of a world out of
which they were being gradually driven ; no more, as Richard
had hoped, an advance post in the great campaign by which the
East was to be humbled before the West.

Hence, no doubt, it is that, notwithstanding the example of
the kingdom of Naples, which was the nearest Catholic neigh-
bour of Cyprus, we find no traces of a Cypriot parliament. There
were councils of nobles and councils of bishops ; there were
high courts and bourgeois courts; and there were, as elsewhere,
three estates well defined, clergy, nobles, and burghers ; but if
there ever was any attempt to range these in an organised body
either for legislation or for money grants, I have failed to dis-
cover it. The ' Bancs,' or ordinances, with which the customs
of the Assizes were supplemented, were issued by the king's
proclamation ; in two or three cases the participation of the
court or of the barons is expressed. In 1362 we have an ordi-
nance issued by the king, Peter I, by the assent of the men of

his court. A few years before, his father, King Hugh, issued his laws by proclamation : " Hear the ban of God and of my Lord the King, Hugh of Lusignan of the Kingdom of Jerusalem and of Cyprus ; know all men that on the 16th of May 1355, the Lord King and his men ordained an assize." Here it is possible there may be some reference to a general court or " witenagemot," but not, I think, to an assembly of estates. According to the Assizes of Jerusalem, every vassal who, whether immediately dependent on the king or on a mesne lord, had done homage to the king as chief lord, was a member of the royal court ; a usage which in so small a state must have crushed out every tendency to representative government [1]. In default of further evidence we must, I think, assume that, as in France before the institution of the states-general, the only check on the king was his court of vassals ; whereas, after the example had been set in the states-general, diets and parliaments of the West, the national life of Cyprus was too much attenuated to allow it to reproduce such institutions on an unfriendly soil. The Basse Cour or Court of Bourgeois, organised under the viscounts or sheriffs of Cyprus, with jurats and other machinery of courts of law, was an organisation of tribunals of justice and local government, not a legislative constitutional organisation : its assizes are therefore a book of procedure rather than a code of laws, and, like the Assizes of the High Court, rather a record of customs than a body of statutes. These courts also, like the court of barons, may be regarded as developments towards constitutional growth, arrested and petrified at a certain stage.

But I have said more than enough upon a subject which, somewhat repulsive by itself, needs severe study before it will begin to be remunerative. The Assizes of Jerusalem will always remain a mine of feudal principles and a treasure to scientific jurists ; they reflect infinite lustre on the Cypriot lawyers who, in an age of turmoil and exertion, continuous and

---

[1] Assizes, i. 254.

overwhelming, found time and labour for recording them. We conceive that the lords of Ibelin must have been well acclimatised in more ways than one ; it is certainly curious that they supplied the main historical support to the kings of Cyprus in marriage, war, and jurisprudence.

King Guy had a very short reign ; and most of the acts that are ascribed to him I have already noted. After the collapse of the third crusade and the three years' truce between Richard and Saladin in 1192, he seems to have retired to Cyprus, and to have died in April 1194 ; the same year the old Emperor Isaac died in the custody of the Hospitallers at Merkeb. Isaac's daughter was still wandering up and down Christendom ; by the agreement for Richard's release she was to have been handed over to Duke Leopold of Austria, her kinsman, but when Baldwin of Bethune brought her to Austria, she found Duke Leopold dead ; she was accordingly brought back to Richard, and subsequently married to a Flemish knight, who came to the East in the fourth crusade in the retinue of John de Neesle, and, in her name, put in a claim for Cyprus, which King Amalric summarily rejected. The rights of Guy devolved upon his brother ; or rather Cyprus, for the reversion of which no arrangements had been made, fell to the lot of the possessor.

Amalric of Lusignan had been, under his brother, constable of both kingdoms and Prince of Tyre ; he was thus in command of such military force as his brother had possessed, and succeeded quietly to his dominion : from Henry VI, as I said, he obtained recognition as king, and was crowned in 1197 ; in 1198 he obtained the crown of Jerusalem, marrying as fourth husband the lady Isabella of Anjou, who had carried the right of succession first to Henfrid of Toron, then to Conrad of Montferrat, and then to Henry of Champagne. The German chancellor, Bishop Conrad of Hildesheim, who had crowned the King of Cyprus, negotiated the marriage and succession, and Amalric, leaving Cyprus under the administration of the Hospitallers, transferred his court to Acre. We hear no more of Cyprus during Amalric's reign. He was an able warrior, and as successful as mere war-like ability, coupled with very indifferent morality towards the infidels, could make him. With the aid of the German crusaders of 1197 he recovered Berytus, where the ceremony of his coronation took place ; he also took Byblus, and besieged Toron ; but the difficulty of keeping terms between the Germans, the Franks, and the military orders, was too great for him. The siege was raised, the Germans retired, and Amalric had to make a truce with Safadin.

The Crusade of Villehardouin passed over without any direct effect on either Cyprus or Palestine. Amalric died at Acre in April, 1205, and was buried in the church of S. Sophia at Nicosia. He left the crown of Cyprus to his eldest son Hugh, the son of his first wife, Eschiva of Ibelin, under the guardianship of Walter of Montbeliard, his brother-in-law. The crown of Jerusalem, the right of which depended on Queen Isabella, was left unclaimed : John of Ibelin, half-brother of Isabella, the uncle of the jurist, was lieutenant of that kingdom ; and he, after some years' searching, found a husband for Mary, the queen's eldest daughter by Conrad of Montferrat ; John of Brienne was accepted as king of Jerusalem in 1210. The queen's second daughter Alice, the child of Henry of Champagne, was given to the young king, Hugh of Cyprus. The event of the minority was a descent made by Walter of Montbeliard on the coast of Asia Minor, the only result of which was booty. Hugh came of age in 1211, and was in that year crowned at Nicosia. His reign was short, and was devoted chiefly to the restoration of order and prosperity in Cyprus. He encouraged the study of law, and was so learned in it himself that Lewis of France applied to him for an opinion on legal procedure, which was held as authoritative by the feudal lawyers. From Palestine he seems to have stood aloof, partly perhaps owing to the fact that the death of Queen Mary, who, dying in 1212, left only an infant daughter, might seem to open the succession to his wife, Queen Alice. In 1217 however he joined the expedition against the fortress of Tabor, persuaded by King Andrew of Hungary, who visited Cyprus on purpose to engage his support. The attempt on Tabor was unsuccessful; and Hugh retired to Tripoli, where he died in February, 1218. It thus happened that neither the great Crusade of 1202 nor the expedition against Damietta in 1219 directly touched the fortunes of Cyprus; for the heir of King Hugh was an infant of nine months old; and the Queen Alice, who with the aid of the child's great uncles, the lords Philip and John of Ibelin, was guardian, seems to have avoided too close alliance with the new troops of Crusaders. Cyprus was, however, a regular station for the pilgrim fleets, and as regularly an object of attack whenever the Sultans saw an opportunity of unresisted devastation.

The little interest of the history runs rapidly on to the Crusade of the Emperor Frederick II, which brought about many other critical conjunctures in the history of Christendom. This particular portion of the history is of no small legal as well as historical interest. The kings of Jerusalem being men of action, practising little self-restraint and never taking care of themselves, generally died young, and left the fate of their kingdom in suspense on the life of their young children. Hence constant minorities, and the need of provisions for guardianship, a need which, as yet, had scarcely begun to be felt in the kingdoms of Europe. The practice therefore of the kingdom of Jerusalem in the matter of regency became a stock of legal cases, which, if not cited as occasion arose in corresponding circumstances in the West, afford to us at least a number of parallels. The earlier practice had been to give the wardship of the person of the heir to the nearest relation incapable of inheriting; that of the kingdom to the presumptive heir [1]. But

---

[1] Assizes, i. 261. If a vassal die the custody of the ward is not to be in the heir, but in the nearest kinsman on the side on which the fief cannot fall. Cf. Glanville, vii. c. 11; Etablissemens, i. c. 117. If he is a sovereign or suzerain, his men shall have care of his body and fortresses, the heir to guard the heritage (i. 435). See Itinerar. R. R. p. xcvii.

the rule laid down in the Assizes, which is really perhaps a generalisation from the earlier cases rather than a deliberate constitution, was that the mother of the heir should be his guardian; in case of her death the next relation on the side on which the kingdom moved, that is, the heir-presumptive; in case no such person could be found, it was for the barons of the kingdom to meet and choose a regent or guardian. The practice seems to have been to leave the queen-mother as regent with a bailiff or high-steward to do the work of government.

In the year 1228 the case in Cyprus was this: the King Henry, although old enough at seven to be crowned, was still a minor. His mother, Queen Alice, had married as a second husband Bohemond V, heir of Antioch, and had quarrelled with the lords of Ibelin, who were not only her nearest relations, but the most powerful and cleverest of the acclimatised baronage. These lords were the sons of that Balian of Ibelin who was supposed, by going to mass instead of to battle, to have ruined the chances of Guy of Lusignan at Nazareth in May, 1187: he had married the widow of King Amalric I, and his sons were thus half-brothers to the many-husbanded Queen Isabella, great-uncles to King Henry, and half-uncles to Queen Alice. So long then as the family party hung together, they formed a strong phalanx; when they quarrelled, all the internal strength of the kingdom was turned against itself. The second marriage of Queen Alice probably broke up the unity. Philip of Ibelin died in 1227; John of Ibelin, lord of Berytus, naturally expected to succeed him as bailiff; the queen proposed a baron named Amalric Barlais. John succeeded in maintaining his position, and became bailiff or regent under the nominal guardianship of the queen. But the struggle was still proceeding when Frederick II, on his way to Palestine, arrived in the Levant. Frederick II, as I need not remind you, was already the "Stupor mundi," the man of unbounded ambition and almost ubiquitous versatility, who never did a great or truly kingly act, or followed any but a selfish aim. He was, as son of Henry VI, heir of imperial aspirations that coveted the whole world, and, as the husband of Yolanda of Brienne, father and guardian of the young heir of Palestine. Yolanda, who must have been a child when she married him, died in this same year 1228, leaving an only son, the luckless Conrad. When then Frederick reached the Peloponnesus, he was met by five Cypriot barons of the queen's party, who asked his aid against the lord of Berytus. The emperor, whether desirous as he might well be to make Cyprus available for military purposes, or simply wishing to assert his right as overlord, undertook to deal with John of Ibelin; the barons told him that the revenues of Cyprus were large enough to secure the conquest of Palestine, and Frederick thought them worth a trial. He arrived at Limasol, and wrote to John as his dearest uncle, begging him to come to him with all his family and concert measures for the crusade. John called together his friends at Nicosia and consulted them : they told him that to admit Frederick was to betray the infant king, but advised him to return a courteous answer, to meet craft with craft. But this John would not do; he swore that he would rather die than let the Crusade fail by his default; and therefore presented himself to the emperor with all his force, and with the little king in his train. Frederick received him ostentatiously, made him change his black mourning robes for scarlet, and entertained him at dinner : after dinner, the usual time apparently for quarrelling, he turned round upon him and insisted on the resignation of the lordship of Berytus, which was a fief of the crown of Jerusalem, and also of the office of bailiff of Cyprus. John boldly told the emperor that this treatment was only what his friends at Nicosia had bidden him expect. The emperor changed colour at the reproach, which showed in what estimation his honour was held. But the friends of the Crusade interfered, and an agreement was made that the question of Berytus should be decided by the high court of Palestine, that of the regency by the high court of Cyprus. This was not carried into effect. John, dreading

the emperor's treachery, fled to Nicosia: there Frederick besieged
him and forced him to a compromise; he did homage for Berytus,
and the emperor was allowed to receive the revenues of Cyprus
until King Henry reached the age of twenty-five, thus apparently
exercising the rights, if not under the name, of an overlord; but
whether he claimed the right as emperor or as king of Jerusalem,
or as representing the nearest kinsman, is not clear [1]. Frederick
left Cyprus under charge of five barons of the island, and went
on to Palestine. After his short stay in the Holy Land, and
his politic but not very far-sighted treaty with the infidels,
he left the East to take care of itself. For about three years
the arrangement continued in force; but in 1231 the emperor's
marshal and deputy, Richard Filangier, tried to wrest Berytus
from John of Ibelin, and threw him into open rebellion. John
equipped a fleet, and, with the young king, landed in Cyprus.
The marshal retired before him. John occupied Famagosta; the
marshal retreated to Nicosia; there he was defeated and forced
to disband his army, which passed over into the service of the
King of Armenia. Cherin held out until Easter, 1233; and then
the last remnant of Frederick's army left Cyprus.

John of Ibelin died in 1236; the imperial power was by that
time broken up in Palestine as well as Cyprus; and now Queen
Alice attempted to turn the tables on Frederick himself. The
relics of the whole Crusading history were imperilled; Frederick
would accept no invitations, nor would he send Conrad to assert
the rights of Yolanda. Alice, therefore, as heir of Jerusalem,
put in her claim for the regency of Palestine; the poor barons
clung to a straw; they accepted her, and she named her third
husband, Ralph of Soissons, bailiff of Jerusalem. No sooner was
he appointed than he left his post and went back to France.
Jerusalem had already fallen to the Sultan of Damascus in 1239;

[1] That Hugh had to perform homage and swear fealty to Frederick II appears from
the letter of Innocent IV, releasing him from the oath in 1247. See Mas-Latrie, Hist.
de Chypre, vol. ii. p. 63. It is said that the barons recognised the emperor as suzerain,
but refused liege homage.

after a brief restoration in 1243, it fell to the Kharismians in 1244; to the Sultan of Egypt in the same year. The crown became a derelict; the title was borne after Conrad by his half-brother Henry, the son of Isabella of England; and subsequently by a number of ruling houses, who seem to have clung to the name far more faithfully than they had ever clung to the reality of the dominion. The remains of substantive power devolved with the title on Hugh the Great, King of Cyprus in 1269.

The rest of the history of King Henry is soon told. He came of age in 1232, married a daughter of the house of Montferrat, and lost her the same year; a second wife, Stephanie of Armenia, died in 1250, and he then married Placentia of Antioch. Henry took a subordinate part in the Crusade of the middle of the century. His action is obscure, as are all the details of the period. In the expedition of 1240 he seems to have borne no part: Richard of Cornwall does not mention a visit to Cyprus either going or returning; but Henry seems to have, in 1246, asserted his right to Jerusalem on the death of his mother, and to have been recognised as king by Innocent IV, who included King Conrad in his father's doom. In the Crusade of S. Lewis, Henry is said by the Cypriot historians to have shared both perils and glories; he certainly received the French king, and entertained him at Nicosia during the winter of 1248, which was so fatal to many of the French nobles. We are not told that King Henry furnished any part of the supplies that S. Lewis collected in Cyprus, the mountains of corn or the towers of wine casks; all these were furnished by the emperor and the Venetians. The King of Cyprus entered Damietta with the French king in triumph in 1249; but he did not, as has been asserted, share his captivity. After this we read no more of him; he died early in 1253, having been the sport of fortune all his life, and leaving the inheritance of his history to a child of a few months old, Hugh II, who reigned from 1253 to 1267.

The only incident of the reign of Hugh II turns, like that in his father's reign, on the question of regency. Queen Placentia

acted as regent, but in the second year of the reign went over to
Palestine and married Balian of Ibelin, the reigning lord of Arsouf.
As Hugh was the last of the Lusignans, the marriage seems to
have been unpopular ; and, either in consequence of it, or after
the death of the queen herself, a new bailiff was appointed. This
was Hugh of Antioch, son of Henry of Antioch, and grandson
of Bohemond IV; his mother Isabella was daughter of King
Hugh I. He was nearest in blood to King Hugh and his presumptive successor. One military exploit signalised the regency:
in 1265 he led to the defence of Acre against the Sultan Bibars
a fleet of Cypriot vessels. Then, says Sanuto, was the military
force of Cyprus in great valour and of great prudence ; there
were in the company 130 knights and much cavalry besides.
The contribution however helped the falling cause but little.
All in Palestine was going to ruin ; already the Venetians and
the Genoese were at war ; the Templars and the Hospitallers
were irreconcilable ; the Frank princes were selling their estates
and returning westward. The lord of Sidon sold, in 1260, Sidon
and Belfort to the Templars ; Balian sold Arsouf to the Hospitallers. Henry of Antioch and his wife claimed the regency
of Palestine as against the house of Brienne. In 1264 Bibars
destroyed Cæsarea ; and the defenders of Acre were obliged, in
self-defence, to lay waste their suburbs, and leave open to the
Saracens the great poliandrum or cemetery of S. Nicolas, in
which 124,000 men had been buried in one year during the third
Crusade. In 1261, the year before Hugh's appointment to the
regency, the Latin empire of Constantinople fell. All the older
medieval things were passing away in both East and West, and
the tide which had led on the Crusades was turning.
    The child king, Hugh II, died in 1267 ; and the bailiff,
Hugh III, succeeded as king. Hugh II was the last of the
house of Lusignan who was left in the East ; in the West there
were still many members of the prolific family. Our memory
recurs most naturally to that large family of the Aliens, the half-
brothers of our king, Henry III, who nine years before had been

banished in consequence of their opposition to the Provisions of Oxford; their father, Hugh X of Lusignan, Count of la Marche, was nephew to the Kings Guy and Amalric. Hugh of Antioch, too, the new king, represented the house of Poictiers, being sprung from Raymond of Poictiers, the uncle of Queen Eleanor, the wife of Henry II. The reigning house of Lusignan in la Marche came to an end in 1303. But although this was the case, the Cypriot dynasty continued to bear the name of Lusignan, to which by a female descent it was entitled; and there are many Lusignans, in England as elsewhere, flourishing at the present day.

Hugh III, the new king, had the advantage of acquiring the throne when he had age and experience to fill it : and he reigned fourteen years, long enough to establish his own authority, and to see the downfall of all the Frank states around him. I will mention three points only in his history; for although he bore the title of the Great, " Hugh the Great," it was a very forlorn hope that he was called on to lead. He seems to have been the king of Cyprus to whom S. Thomas Aquinas dedicated the famous treatise " De Regimine Principum;" a book which, owing to the great reputation of its author, and the definiteness of the principles which it enunciates, became a handbook of the relations of Church and State in the middle ages. Of the work which we now possess under this name, only a book and a half out of the four books was the work of S. Thomas, the rest was added probably by Ptolemy of Lucca ; but the book itself was a model which later publicists chose to follow or to comment upon. Many of these commentaries are found in our libraries; and down to the age of Sir John Fortescue, the book addressed to the King of Cyprus occupied a position of authority inferior only to the Politics of Aristotle. It is not improbable that the book was originally written for the education of the young King Hugh II ; but it is certainly very curious that the composition both of the great Feudal Code of the Assizes, and of the manual of medieval politics, should have a direct relation to this remote little island. The second point to be noted is this :—

Hugh saw nearly all the Crusading conquests lost. In 1268 Antioch was taken, and the prince, Bohemond VI, retired to Tripoli. In 1269 Hugh claimed the crown of Jerusalem, and was crowned at Tyre on the 24th of September. But this empty honour was not obtained without competition. The king's great-aunt, Mary of Antioch, daughter of Bohemond IV and grand-daughter of King Amalric, contested the title ; she carried her cause to Rome for the arbitration of the pope ; and unable to make good any claim herself, she sold in 1277 her rights to Jerusalem to Charles of Anjou, the King of Naples, the brother of S. Lewis, and head of that Angevin house which transmitted the crowns of Jerusalem and Sicily to René of Anjou, the father-in-law of our King Henry VI. Hugh III then was King of Jerusalem when Edward I made his crusade. In May 1271, and for several months later, the two kings were together at Acre; and during their intimacy Hugh put before Edward a question which bore a signally close relation to that on which so much of the interest of Edward's own reign was to turn. The documents concerning it are preserved among the Assizes of Jerusalem. Unfortunately we have only the case, not the opinion which Edward gave. The question was, what obligation lay on the knights of Cyprus to feudal service within the kingdom of Jerusalem ; exactly parallel to the great question of 1297 in England, upon which the Confirmation of Charters resulted.

It was not decided by Edward, but John of Ibelin had laid down the rule : " Three things are they bound to do out-side the realm for the lord ; 1. For the marriage of him or any of his children; 2. To guard and defend his faith and honour; 3. Por le besoing aparant de sa seignorie ou le comun profit de sa terre." When we find a jurist named Accursi d'Arezzo practising at Acre in 1270, it becomes even probable that Edward picked up his friend Francesco there. It was possibly on this occasion that Edward laid down the rule that, for the recovery of the East, Egypt should be first occupied, then the Holy

Land, and then Constantinople. When that was done, and not till then, would the Christian warriors, settled and established, be able to dwell safely. So at least says Marino Sanuto writing in 1321.

But neither Edward's little army nor his legal skill could save King Hugh from discomfiture; in 1272 he was forced to submit to make a treaty with Bibars, which left him only Acre and the right of pilgrimage to Nazareth, and for this he had to thank, it was said, the diplomacy of Edward. After Edward's departure, and an attempt to sustain the Frank cause in Tripoli, Hugh seems to have devoted himself to the care of his island kingdom, which was itself threatened by the monstrous policy of Charles of Anjou. That wretched tyrant, by way of inaugurating his purchased sovereignty, wrested Acre from King Hugh in 1277. He did not live to recover it. After a siege of four months the Cypriot knights declared their term of service at an end, and the siege was raised. Hugh was a patron of learned men, and a founder of monasteries. Probably he saw that unless the Christians were unanimous he must be content to sit still. The Hospitallers supported him; the Templars spited him; the Genoese helped him; the Venetians thwarted him. So he stayed in Cyprus, where the people to a great extent prospered under his care, and had sons and daughters. His wife was a lady of the house of Ibelin: he died at Tyre in 1284; he was buried in the abbey of Lapais. His eldest son, John I, who succeeded him, died in 1285; his brother and successor, Henry II, reigned from 1285 to 1324; witnessing a period of transitional history which affected the East as well as the West, and which furnishes material of more curious if not wider interest.

So long as Acre held out against the Infidels, that is exactly a hundred years from the date when Richard restored it to Christendom, almost all the living interest of the Crusades centres in that curious stronghold; for it must have been a very strange encampment of fighting and praying men of all nations. There each of the great orders had its strong tower, palace, and appointed share of the wardship of the walls. There the Hospitallers and the Templars issued from their palaces the orders that governed their brethren throughout Christendom; the Genoese and the Pisans had their quarters in close neighbourhood; the Venetians had their Tower far off, between the Tower of the English and the ward of the Hospitallers; and the mendicant orders had each their house and church to themselves. Immensely strong, and able to draw in supplies constantly from the sea, Acre was a standing menace to the Eastern world; but without were fightings and within were fears. The very closeness in which the conflicting powers were encamped intensified the dangers of their disunion. There was still great appearance of strength; the King of Jerusalem and Cyprus was at least safe in the castle around which this fortified camp was spread; all along the coast northwards, of Syria and Armenia, were placed the strong munitions of the military orders; over the sea, a little way, was Cyprus, the great granary of Palestine, and within the lines of Palestine itself were strongholds of both the knights and the "pullani," or acclimatised Franks, which were fortified with great skill, and need indeed succumb to nothing short of famine. All this, however far short it fell of a well-administered state or well-regulated camp, was still a strong power when the fatal quarrels in the West, the downfall of the Hohenstaufen, the wicked policy of Charles of Anjou, the rivalry of the Venetians and the Genoese, combined to bring about the end.

Acre held out almost to the last; Antioch had fallen in 1268; all Palestine proper, save Acre and the road to Nazareth, had been surrendered in 1272; Tripoli was lost in 1289. Dependent on Acre were Tyre, Sidon, and Berytus, and a few straggling forts that must fall when Acre fell. That was on the 18th of May, 1291. The King of Jerusalem and Cyprus at the time was Henry II, the second son of Hugh III, who had succeeded his brother John in 1285, and had been duly crowned in 1286. The recovery of Acre from the forces of the King of Naples, which was effected before he could duly receive the crown of

E 2

Jerusalem, was the one brilliant exploit of a long and otherwise unhappy reign. The assistance which the military orders afforded him on the occasion caused the regent of Naples to confiscate all the estates of those orders within the kingdom of Naples, which formed a precedent for the atrocious measures of Philip the Fair against the Templars. Five years afterwards the Sultan Khalil Ashraf besieged Acre : King Henry brought his forces to the rescue, but, on the day of the assault by the Mussulmans, lost heart and sailed away. For three days the luckless defenders struggled and perished, and on the fourth day the city was taken. I shall not dwell on the valour of the knights or on the atrocities of the captors. The same day at evening the Franks of Tyre embarked and set sail for the West. The Templars left Sidon and went to Cyprus ; and the people of Berytus surrendered. The break up of the great camp was followed by a dispersion of the forces of the Cross. The kingdom of Armenia began to falter in its obedience to the Roman Church. The Armenian Catholicos had to flee from Mesopotamia to Sis in 1292 ; and about the same time the relics of Antiochene chivalry took service under the Armenian king. The military orders were only kept in Cyprus by the gift of Limasol, which King Henry bestowed on them conjointly; but soon the Templars sought their Western preceptories, within a very few years to perish utterly; the Teutonic knights found work in the conversion of the North ; the Hospitallers, maintaining a better heart, fitted out a new Crusade, and in 1308 seized the island of Rhodes, whence for two hundred and fifteen years they made the Mediterranean too hot to hold a Turkish fleet. The rest of the unattached Franks found a home in Cyprus.

Amongst these was one little known and obscure knightly order, which Englishmen need not be ashamed to recognise ; the Order of the Knights of S. Thomas of Acre. This was a little body of men who had formed themselves into a semi-religious order on the model of the Hospitallers. In the third Crusade, one William, an English priest, chaplain to Ralph de

Diceto, Dean of S. Paul's, had devoted himself to the work of burying the dead at Acre, as the Hospitallers had given themselves at first to the work of tending the sick. He had built himself a little chapel there, and bought ground for a cemetery; like a thorough Londoner of the period, he had called it after S. Thomas the Martyr; and, somehow or other, as his design was better known, the family of the martyr seem to have approved of it; the brother-in-law and sister of Becket became founders and benefactors, and a Hospital of S. Thomas the Martyr of Canterbury, of Acre, was built in London itself on the site of the house where the martyr was born [1]. Little indeed is known of the early days of the knights; they were not numerous, and probably poor; but when Peter des Roches, the Bishop of Winchester and ex-justiciar, was in Palestine in 1231, he placed them in a new church and under the rule of the Templars, giving them also in his will a legacy of 500 marks [2]. They had their proper dress and cross: according to Favin their habit was white, and the cross a full red cross charged with a white scallop; but the existing cartulary of the order describes the habit simply as a mantle with a cross of red and white [3]. They were building a new church when Edward was at Acre; and in 1278 we find him writing to the King of Cyprus on their behalf [4]. The Chronicle of the Teutonic knights, in relating the capture of

---

[1] In the ninth year of John, Oct. 13, 1207, messengers of the house of S. Thomas at Acre, being canons, had a safe-conduct. They had come to England to seek alms for the redemption of captives; Rot. Pat. ed. Hardy, i. 76. The "Terra Sancti Thomæ" abutted on the land of the Temple at Casale Album, near Coquet; Paoli, Cod. Dipl. S. Joh., i. 468. Richard, the English tanner, at Acre, in 1273 sold two houses in the Street of the Tannery to the Hospitallers; ib. 195, 196.
[2] Matthew Paris, ed. Wats, p. 472.
[3] MS. Cotton, Tiberius C. V.
[4] Mas-Latrie, Hist. de Chypre, ii. 81, 82, where two documents are printed from the letters of Edward in the Public Record Office. In one of these the king commends Ralph de Coumbe, master of the Hospital of S. Thomas, to the good offices of Hugh of Lusignan, in Cyprus; in another, dated Sept. 15, 1279, Ralph de Cardolio and the brethren write to the king on the misfortunes of Palestine, and urge that the master of the Order should be sent into Syria. See the 7th Report of the Deputy Keeper of the Records, App. II. No. 2252; Royal Letters, MS. (Chancery), No. 4260.

Acre, places the knights of S. Thomas at the head of the 5000 soldiers whom the king of England had sent to Palestine[1], and Hermann Corner, who however wrote a century later, mentions them amongst the defenders of Acre. We know from their cartulary that they had lands in Yorkshire, Middlesex, Surrey, and Ireland[2]; their Master was called Master of the whole Order of the Knighthood of S. Thomas the Martyr, in the kingdom of Cyprus, Apulia, Sicily, Calabria, Brundusium, England, Flanders, Brabant, Scotland, Wales, Ireland, and Cornwall. Some few noble names of the masters have been preserved; Ralph of Coumbe was master in or about 1278[3], Henry de Bedford in 1323, and Robert de Kendale in 1344. In 1350 the order was recognised as still existing by the German traveller Ludolf of Suchen.

---

[1] Matthæi, Vet. Ævi Analecta, x. 182 ; Eccard, Scriptores, i. 942.

[2] At Wapping, Plumstead, Coulsdon, and Doncaster. The estate at Wapping was the gift of Tierri of Alegate ; MS. Cott. fo. 156. Coulsdon was confirmed to the master of the knights by a charter of Henry III, in 1261 ; fo. 236 : the Hospital of S. James, at Doncaster, was given by Peter de Mauley : " Deo et militiæ beati Thomæ martyris de Acon ;" fo. 258 : the benefactors in Ireland are enumerated by Edward I in a grant of confirmation, 5th June, A°. 17 ; Fulk de Villars, John de la Zouche, Edmund Bret, Gilbert Marshall, Walter Marshall, and Philip Horsey. James Butler, Earl of Ormond, was another at a later date.

[3] Frater Radulfus preceptor fratrum Sancti Thomæ de Acon in Anglia ; A.D. 1249. William of Huntingfield "magister militiæ hospitalis B. Thomæ Martyris de Acon Londini ;" MS. Cotton, fo. 166. Richard of Southampton was master of the Hospital, 11 Edw. II ; Thomas de Sallowe, "magister domus," 40 Edw. III.

Aug. 7, 1323, Henry de Bedford, master general of the order, creates John de Paris prior and custos of the Chapel of S. Nicholas of Nicosia ; sealing with his seal for Cyprus.

June 17, 1324, William de Glastingebury, preceptor of the house of S. Thomas of Acre, in the diocese of Nicosia, with consent of the chapter of the house, to wit, Nicolas Clifton, John of Paris, and William of S. Bartholomew, appoints Nicolas Clifton proctor against a brother Henry, who calls himself master ; "actum Nicosiæ in capella Sancti Nicolai presentibus Henrico et Thoma presbyteris Anglicis et prædicto Johanne priore dictæ capellæ."

Aug. 30, 1344, Robert Kendale, master of the whole order, appoints Henry of Colchester and William of Brunill to collect money for the order ; "dat. Nicosiæ" in the house of Guddefrid, archdeacon of the church of Famagosta, vicar of Philip, archbishop of Nicosia.

Feb. 2, 1357, Hugh Curteys invests Richard of Tickhill ; "actum in regno Cypri in Nicosia intra ecclesiam Beati Nicolai Anglicorum, præsentibus Francisco de Gave burgensi Nicosiæ, domino Rob. de Swillington canonico, domino Ricardo de Chatesby presbytero Anglico ; Guillelmo Gaston de Anglia Turcopolo regis et pluribus aliis."

In 1357 Hugh de Curteys, the preceptor of Cyprus, invested one Richard of Tickhill with the habit of the order, in the presence of Robert Swillington, canon, Sir Richard Chatesby, an English priest, and William Gaston of England, Turcopolier to the king of Cyprus. The ceremony was performed in the church of S. Nicolas of the English in the city of Nicosia; one of the many churches which formerly, according to Father Stephen of Lusignan, adorned that city, but of which any relic would now, since the Venetians destroyed 130 in the process of fortification, scarcely be looked for. The hospital in London became, probably at the fall of the Templars, a mere Augustinian Hospital. Its church, or one built on the site of it, is now the chapel of the Mercers' Company[1].

England had not, with all her business under Henry III and Edward I, forgotten Palestine: some of her sons fell at Acre, and the remnant of the little order found a home at Nicosia. But the great king himself never forgot his first love; in fact all the nobler Plantagenets, Richard of Cornwall, Edward I, Henry of Lancaster, Henry of Bolingbroke, Henry V, and Cardinal Beaufort, all either made the pilgrimage or looked forward to a great crusade. To Edward I, in or about 1303, was addressed the very amusing "Libellus de recuperatione Terræ Sanctæ[2]," the work of an ecclesiastical judge in Aquitaine, whose name is unknown, but who speculates like a special correspondent of the period; a book which shows a just sense of the evils which had rendered the united action of Christendom impossible; points out ways in which all political dangers in Europe can be avoided; stigmatises the crime of war between Christian princes, the ruinous discord between Venice, Pisa, and Genoa, and proposes to settle the military orders chiefly in Cyprus, and employ

---

[1] The history of the London house may be read in Newcourt, Repertorium, i. 553; and Mon. Angl. vi. 645 : it must be carefully distinguished from the Hospital of S. Thomas the Martyr in Southwark, the germ of the present S. Thomas's Hospital. See also Itinerarium Regis Ricardi, præf. pp. cxii–cxiii.

[2] Printed at the end of the second volume of Bongars' *Gesta Dei per Francos.*

them in the recovery of the holy places. Curiously enough, one of the remedial measures proposed by the writer, who is especially strong on the subject of natural science, is that girls should be taught to practise medicine and surgery; they are to learn grammar, and logic also, natural principles, and mathematics, but it is that they may qualify as wives for the Oriental princes.

But to return to Cyprus : Edward, as I said, was not the only one of his family who remembered it : Henry III had proposed to the Bishop of Bethlehem a marriage between his son Edmund and the queen-mother Placentia in 1256; the young king was also to marry one of his daughters[1]. The records however both of that reign and the next contain more references to Armenia than to Cyprus; thus in 1260 Alexander IV exhorts Edward to defend Armenia against the Tartars; in 1280 the Bishop of Hebron, vicegerent of the patriarch, sends the thanks of the Franks, and adds that Armenia and Cyprus have been laid waste by a plague of locusts[2]; the same intelligence is sent by the master of S. Thomas from Acre; the wars of Charles of Anjou cut off all hope of succour, and the king of the Tartars had demanded provisions from Acre. Boniface VIII was unwearied in impressing on England the importance of these regions; in 1298 he urges the sending of a subsidy to Sembat king of Armenia[3]; in 1300 he is negotiating a general confederacy which will include the princes of Armenia and Georgia. Edward cannot do much, but if he cannot send knights he will send missionaries. The king of the Tartars sends envoys to him, and one of them is baptized. The last measures of Edward I and the first of Edward II are to the same purpose. Edward I issues safe-conduct to the bishop of Lydda and other Dominicans who are going to convert the heathen ; Edward II sends a warning to the king of the Tartars against Mahometanism. The kings of Armenia, who have apparently little else to do, send constant appeals for money. Faithful Armenia, says Sanuto,

---

[1] Fœd. i. 341.   [2] Ib. 402, 586.   [3] Ib. 900, 742, 749, 902, 919.

writing in 1321, lies among the wild beasts; on one side the lion, the Tartar; on another the leopard, the Sultan; on a third the wolf, the Turks; on the fourth the serpent, the Corsairs. But these I must notice by and by.

Henry II of Cyprus reigned nominally from 1285 to 1324; but during great part of the time he was superseded by one or other of his brothers: his quarrels with them form the whole history of his reign; at one time he was a prisoner in Armenia, whither his brother, Amalric, the prince of Tyre, had sent him; another brother, Guy, the constable of Cyprus, was put to death by his orders for a conspiracy against him. The Popes were much exercised by this fraternal strife; but it was not until after the death of Guy that Henry had peace. As so often happens after an unquiet reign, he outlived all his enemies, and died rather regretted than not. This was in 1324: he was buried in the church of the Franciscans at Nicosia. When he had been able to exercise independent authority he had used it well; he had welcomed the refugees from Acre and fortified Famagosta; he contributed largely to the judicial decisions which form the supplement to the Assizes, and he established a strong judicature in Cyprus. But he was an epileptic, which perhaps accounts for his incapacity to retain the rule; and he left no children.

With the accession of his nephew, Hugh IV, begins a more stirring and, perhaps, the most interesting period of the Cypriot history. Before however entering on the outline of this portion of our subject, we may just look back to Armenia, where the native kingdom and the native dynasty were nearly coming to an end. Leo I, the first king, who was regarded by the Armenian writers as a really great and patriotic ruler, died in 1219, leaving an infant daughter who carried the crown to her husbands in succession; Philip of Antioch first, who, failing to make himself agreeable on the Church question to the native lords, especially a great lord called Constantius, or Constantine, was put to death with his partisans. The second husband was Hayton, the son of Constantius, who reigned for nearly fifty

F

years, at first under his father's directions, and after the year
1237 independently. Hayton was thus king during the whole
of the crusading period of the thirteenth century, and had
dealings with Lewis IX in his first Crusade, and with Edward
of England during his stay in Palestine. He was moreover
the king of Armenia in whose time Marco Polo set out on his
travels in Asia; and it was through his means that the Western
kings became acquainted with the Tartar dynasty at Samarcand
and its tendencies to favour Christianity. For the Tartar rulers
during this period were far from being committed to Islam;
they received and favoured missions and protected Christian
doctrines in a liberal fashion, without understanding or finally
committing themselves [1]. Hayton may possibly have the credit
of having stirred up the Mongols against the Khalifate of
Bagdad, which Hulaku brought to an end in 1259. The
alliance with the Tartars brought down the Sultan of Egypt on
Armenia; and, after the capture of Antioch, Hayton resigned his
throne and retired to a monastery, where he took the name of
Macarius, and died soon after. His brother, the constable of
Armenia, Sempad, Sembat, or Sinibald, was the author of an
Armenian chronological history of authority. A better known
person, also of the royal house, was the monk Hayton, who
about the year 1305 wrote a history called the Flower of the
Histories of the East. Hayton's career is curious. He had
been lord of Gorigos, or Corycus, on the Mediterranean coast,
and had both fought in Palestine and negotiated among the
Tartars, where the Armenian princes were constantly tantalised
with the hope of converting the khans. About 1290 he went
to Cyprus and became a Præmonstratensian canon, as Brother

---

[1] Mosheim in his " Historia Tartarorum " has collected all the notices accessible in
his time of the attempts to convert the Tartars, which for a long time had a show of
success. After dallying with Christianity, the Khans seem to have become finally
Mahometan and hostile at the beginning of the 14th century. But the subject, since
the publication of the Armenian authorities, has become susceptible of much more
elucidation.

Antony. From Cyprus he turned westward and came to France, where the Pope was. It was at Poictiers that he dictated his history, which accordingly was written in Latin. It has been printed both in Latin and in a French translation of the same century, but contains more about the Tartars than about the Franks. It is not improbable that to Hayton's influence we may trace some of the interest shown in Armenia by Edward I and Edward II.

King Hayton, however, who died in 1271, was succeeded on the Armenian throne by his son Leo II, who seems to have clung to the Tartar alliance as against Egypt, and to have come to an open rupture with the Pope on the other side. He was likewise in close alliance with Byzantium, and, although his history is obscure, he seems to have asserted an independent position for which his successors toiled in vain. He reigned eighteen years, and was followed by four of his sons in succession. Of these Hayton II purchased the support of the West by reconciling himself and his people to Rome; he was a poet and historian also, and ended in becoming a Franciscan as Friar John. With his brother, Thoros, who on his withdrawal became king, he went to Constantinople to obtain help from Andronicus Paleologus. On their return they found themselves unseated by a third brother, Sembat; fled to Cyprus first and then to Tartary, but were taken; Hayton was blinded and Thoros strangled. Sembat had thrown over the Roman alliance and been crowned by the Armenian Catholicos; but, finding the Saracens still gaining ground, he changed his tactics, and obtained from Boniface VIII a bull for a subsidy, which was circulated in England in 1298 [1]. He was supplanted in his turn by his brother Constantius. He, after a short reign, was succeeded by Leo III, son of Thoros, who reigned under the guardianship of his uncle, the blind brother John, who had been king as Hayton II. Both Leo and his uncle were put to death

---

[1] Fœd. i. 900.

F 2

by a Tartar general, at the suggestion, according to the Roman writers, of the discontented Armenians, who had been again too summarily reconciled to the papacy in a council at Sis, in 1307. Oissim, who succeeded in 1308, was another son of Leo II. He was connected with the Cypriot history, taking part with the brothers of King Henry against him; and he also obtained a confirmation of the union with the Roman Church in 1316. Leo IV, who was the last of the native dynasty, succeeded his father Oissim in 1320. His whole reign was a continued struggle against the Moslems, who were encroaching on every side, and his name became very well known in the West. It was in his defence that John XXII proclaimed a Crusade in 1333; and among other helps Edward III, in 1335, allowed his ambassadors £40 from the London subsidy. Leo found himself before his death reduced to the few mountain fortresses from which his ancestors had emerged two centuries before. He failed to gain the support of the Armenians, and was thus thrown on that of the Latins, who could really give him no aid. He was assassinated about 1342, and his dynasty ended with him. The five remaining Kings of Armenia sprang from a branch of the Cypriot house of Lusignan, and were little more than Latin exiles in the midst of several strange populations all alike hostile.

We have now to return to Hugh IV, King of Cyprus, a prince who is known in literary history as the king to whom Boccaccio dedicated his genealogy of the gods. He reigned twenty-five years, and has the merit of setting on foot the great alliance between the Venetians, the Pope, and the Knights of Rhodes, to which the chief successes of his reign and that of his son were due. It is true that these successes wear to modern eyes the look of mere piratical exploits: but we have two points to remember in this connexion. All naval war, not only during the middle ages, but down to the seventeenth century, was more or less piratical; and the war between the Christians and the Saracens, although interrupted now and then by truces, which both parties felt ashamed to make and took the first opportunity of breaking, was really continuous and internecine. The coasts of Asia Minor had been gradually lost to the Christians; the coasts of Egypt were to some extent open to reprisals. The fact that the coast of Syria and Palestine afforded so few harbours had, when once the fortified harbour of Acre had fallen into the hands of the Saracens, the effect of removing the seat of war to the Asiatic and Egyptian coasts. That was the deliberate opinion of King Edward I, who had ruled that Egypt must be the first point of attack, then Palestine, and then Constantinople. Hence the two attacks on Damietta in 1219 and 1249. Now, after a long period of defence, the Christians took the initiative. The leaders and fighters in all this from 1308 to 1523 were the Knights of Rhodes, but Cyprus was very frequently the head-quarters and source of supplies, and the Western pilgrims were not chary of labour, blood, or treasure. In all the great achievements of the time too some English pilgrims were associated. The single exploit however of King Hugh's reign was a descent on Smyrna in 1344. John of Biandra, Grand Prior of Lombardy, the head of the expedition, made himself master of the citadel; and Smyrna remained in the hands of the knights until the close of the century. The King of Cyprus had contributed a contingent towards the fleet, but, except by weakening the Saracen power a little, he obtained no immediate benefit for his state [1].

The great plague of 1349 fell with especial fatality on Cyprus; only one castle, that of Dieudamour, was safe for the king to dwell in; and the island got such a reputation for unwholesome air that the trade almost ceased. The Frank population especially diminished. In 1349 the traveller, Ludolf of Suchen, described the

---

[1] Paoli, Cod. Dipl. Ord. S. Joh. ii. 93, gives a commission from the Pope to the Archbishop of Candia to recover from the King of Cyprus, the Grand-Master of Rhodes and the Doge of Venice, the money covenanted for the defence of Smyrna.

barons of Cyprus as the richest in the world. After the plague
Hugh had to recruit the ranks of the nobles by conferring titles on
the merchant class. The succours sought in Europe were only
scantily afforded. The King of Armenia cried louder and got more
sympathy than the King of Cyprus. Still some brave men went
out to the East. It is at least to this period that we have to refer
the pilgrimage and warlike exploits of Henry of Lancaster, the
great duke-palatine and father-in-law of John of Gaunt. He,
according to his biographer Capgrave, about the year 1351 made
his grand tour, and fought not only in Prussia, where he went
first, but also in Rhodes, Cyprus and the East, ending his military
education with a campaign in Granada. William Lord Roos of
Hamlake died in 1352, either in Palestine or in Cyprus, on a more
distinctly religious pilgrimage : to 1357 we have referred our last
glimpse of the English order and their church at Nicosia. In
1352 Henry Lord Percy left by will 1000 marks sterling in florins
of Florence for his son Henry to make the pilgrimage. But the
French war in the West, and the struggles of the Venetians with
the Genoese, prevented anything like national or united expeditions. In the midst of turmoil King Hugh died in 1359, and
was buried in the Blackfriars' church at Nicosia. His eldest son,
Guy, prince of Galilee and constable of Cyprus, had died before
him, leaving a son, Hugh of Lusignan. He on his grandfather's
death went into the West to obtain some support in his claim on
the crown, which, owing to the fact that representation was not
allowed by the laws of Cyprus, failed to obtain recognition.
This is that Hugh of Cyprus whom the Pope in 1360 made sena-
tor of Rome, and who really ruled there from January to August
1361. He has been confounded by some of the Cypriot historians with his grandfather, who accordingly is made to abdicate
and die at Rome. Hugh, having failed to find employment for
his military genius at Rome, resigned the senatorship, and we
hear no more of him [1].

---

[1] Gregorovius, Gesch. d. St. Rom., vi. 393 ; Theiner, Diplom. S. Sedis, ii. 391.

The crown of Cyprus had been secured by Hugh IV to his second son Peter, whom he had had crowned, before his death, at Nicosia.

Peter, with apparently some characteristics of genius, had several more or less allied to insanity. He had made a vow of slaughter against all Mussulmans generally, and, for the purpose of keeping it, wore his naked sword hung round his neck. Our acquaintance with him is largely due to Froissart, who follows his exploits with some minuteness ; but we have a more valuable record in the work written by Philip de Mazzeriis, chancellor of Cyprus, on the life of the legate Peter Thomas, whose period of activity nearly coincides with the reign of King Peter, 1361–1369[1]. Peter Thomas was a native of Guienne, a born subject of Edward III, and was probably instrumental personally in creating the interest felt in England and Guienne in the plans of the King of Cyprus. He crowned Peter at Famagosta, and made an attempt to bring over the Greek population of Cyprus to the Roman obedience. The first exploit of King Peter was the voyage across the enchanted gulf to Satalia, and the capture of the place, where, as Froissart tells us, he slew without exception all the inhabitants of both sexes whom he found there. In this expedition he was assisted not only by the Catalans and the fleet of Rhodes, but by an English force, or a force under an English knight, whom the Italian historians name Robert of Toulouse[2], and describe as sent into Armenia to demand tribute from the princes. If Robert of Toulouse was engaged in the sack of Satalia, we must hope for our national credit's sake, that he was only an Englishman by courtesy, a Knight of Rhodes of the langue of England, which would contain knights drawn from the continental estates of the Plantagenets. Having fleshed his maiden sword at Satalia, King Peter set out on a mission westward, a general canvass of Christendom. Having gone by way

---

[1] Acta Sanctorum Boll. Jan. ii. 995–1023.
[2] The name is variously given : Dulaurier reads it Lusugnan ; it also appears as Julassan, which looks like a corruption of an English name.

of Rhodes to Venice, the legate, making known the approach
of the king, applied for succour to the "communitates, dominos
et tyrannos" of Lombardy, and then passed on to Avignon.
In March 1363, King Peter himself reached Avignon, where
the Pope gladly received him, and determined to preach a new
Crusade, of which King John of France, who had just emerged
from his prison in England, should be the leader. After settling
this, the king went to Prague, where he saw the emperor
Charles IV, and so to Juliers, Brussels and Bruges. Every-
where he was received with suppers and tournaments, in both
of which he seems to have played his part. Whilst he was
enjoying himself, the legate was negotiating, and it was determined that the Crusade under King John should start from
Marseilles in the following March. Froissart follows the movements of King Peter through Picardy to Calais, and on to
London. At London he was well entertained; Queen Philippa
made him handsome presents; King Edward gave him a ship
named the Catharine. The mayor, Henry Picard, gave him
a dinner, and allowed him to win fifty marks at play: but as
the poor king did not lose with a good grace, the mayor gave
him his money back again. Of substantial aid he got little;
and Edward was not liberal even with promises; he himself
was too old to go, but his sons and nobles might. Peter went
back therefore to France. Before he went he was robbed by
some English highwaymen; as however Edward paid all his
expenses, he was probably no great loser.

King John had during this time returned to England, where
he took part in the festivities, but died soon after, in April 1364,
thus putting an end to one part of the great design; and one of
Peter's first acts after returning through Guienne to Paris, was
to attend King John's funeral, May 7, 1364, and the coronation
of his successor. He seems then to have revisited the emperor
and the kings of Hungary and Poland, a route which hindered
him from reaching Venice until the legate had left. The legate
had been called away to Cyprus to settle a quarrel between the

Genoese and King Peter's officers. Peter appeared at Venice rather forlorn; but he had obtained the support of some English lords, one of whom, the Earl of Warwick, must, if the traditions of the Beauchamps are to be trusted, have gone on before him; for in the great battle in Turkey, fought Nov. 1, 1364, he took prisoner a son of the King of Lithuania, whom he brought back to England and made a Christian. Two other Englishmen of distinction are known to have followed Peter; John Lord Grey of Codnor, and a knight of the house of Stapylton, who had been especially impressed by the virtues of the legate.

Having got together as many volunteers as he could, and a considerable fleet, King Peter sailed from Venice and joined the fleet of the Hospitallers. The great stroke to be made was the capture of Alexandria. This was effected with no small bloodshed and very rich spoils. Alexandria taken, the next object was to strengthen the fortifications and make it the head-quarters of a Crusade. But here the English auxiliaries objected. There can be no doubt that the story is true, for it is from the pen of the legate himself: they refused even to stay all night in Alexandria, and having conspired with a certain prince, whose name the legate feels bound to keep secret, set sail for Cyprus. They sent word home too that the city was only half taken[1]. It was a great disappointment to the ardent crusaders; but no doubt the English lords who had had experience in foreign warfare saw that Alexandria was untenable, and the season, for it was now the 10th of October, 1365, was too far advanced. The failure of the Crusade was bitterly commented on by Petrarch, who in a letter to Boccaccio writes, at the time, in the severest way of the greediness and irresolution of the Transalpines[2],

---

[1] "Recesserunt Anglici qui videbantur fortiores, facta conspiratione cum principe cujus ex parentela et dolosa sequela nomen tacere debeo;" P. de Mazz. AA. SS. l. c. p. 1016.

[2] "Siquidem Petrus Cypri rex Alexandriam cepit in Egypto, magnum opus et memorabile nostræque religionis in immensum amplificandæ fundamentum ingens, si quantum ad capiendam tantum ad servandam urbem animi fuisset; qui certe non defuit, ut fama, nisi comitatus ejus ex transalpinis maxime gentibus collectus, meliori-

G

and many years after laments, in an epistle to Philip de Mazzeriis, the loss to Christendom, and the wretched effect produced, by the failure, on the character and fate of the king [1]. The English lords seem to have stayed sometime longer in Cyprus: the legate died at Famagosta in January, 1366, and they brought back to England the biography by Philip the Chancellor, which has furnished the most certain details of the story. After the Alexandrian expedition the Venetians, whose commerce was suffering, prevailed on Peter to treat for a peace with Egypt, which was to establish Cypriot consulates and reduce the customs in the ports of the Levant; but the attempt failed. The next year, with the Genoese and the Hospitallers, he ravaged the Syrian coast, but again had to make peace. He then visited Rome in search of succour, and returned finally to Cyprus in September 1368. The rest of King Peter's life was very wretched: he had left his queen during his long visit to the West, and she had proved faithless: he retaliated on the nobles who had been her favourites, and gave rein to his cruelty and lasciviousness. If he were not mad, as seems most probable, he was desperate; and his family took the lead in getting rid of him. He was assassinated by a body of nobles, who acted with the concurrence of his brother John, the prince of Antioch, on the 16th of January, 1369. His wife was Eleanor of Aragon; and it was this connexion, no doubt, that gave him a higher place than his predecessors had enjoyed in the estimation of the Western kings.

Peter II, who succeeded him, was a boy of thirteen; his uncle John acted as regent. Peter reigned till 1382. He avenged his father's death by murdering his uncle in 1375. His reign witnessed a fatal rupture between the Venetians and Genoese, which accelerated the fate of Cyprus. The representatives of

---

bus semper ad principia rerum quam ad exitus, illum in medio præstantissimi operis deserentes, ut qui pium regem non pietate sed cupiditate sequentes, collectis spoliis abiere piique voti impotem avari voti compotes fecere;" Petrarch, Opp. p. 843; Ep. Senil. lib. 8. ep. 8.

[1] Ib. Lit. 13. ep. 2: "Petrus rex Cypri, indigni vir exitus sed sacræ memoriæ nisi," &c.

the two republics quarrelled about precedence at the coronation : the court decided in favour of Venice. This was complicated by a quarrel between the queen-mother and the prince of
Antioch. The Genoese took up arms and overran the whole
island. The boy king was taken prisoner, and to secure his
ransom had to pledge Famagosta to the Genoese. This great
city and the port, which Sir John Mandeville thought the finest
in the world, was permanently lost to the kings, for it was subsequently made over to the Genoese altogether in order to obtain
the release of James, the king's uncle and successor, who had
been detained as a hostage by the admiral Fregoso.

The particular interest which attaches to the struggle of Venice
and Genoa, a struggle which only ended when the Levant was
left to the Turks, and was one great cause of the abridgment of
Christendom at the close of the middle ages, and the glorious
exploits of the knights of Rhodes, however close to our subject,
are far too wide and engrossing topics to be discussed inciden-
tally. But the fate of Armenia, where the very succession of
the kings is very obscure, demands a word. The first Latin
king, according to the native historians, was John of Lusignan,
also called Constantine, who reigned only a year ; his brother, Guy
of Lusignan, who succeeded in 1343, was connected by marriage with the Cantacuzenes, and even addressed Edward III as
cousin [1]. Both the brothers were little else than adventurers.
Guy reigned for only three years. In 1347 his successor Constantius, or Constantine, was, through an envoy of the same
name, collecting money in England by virtue of a brief issued
by Clement VI [2]. He seems to be identical with Constantine,
who, in 1351, was on the throne ; in his favour also alms were
collected in England. He died in 1361. After an interval of three
years, during which the crown was offered to Peter of Cyprus, and
an unknown fourth king may possibly have reigned, Leo V appears
on the throne in 1365. He had a hard fight for it ; from 1371 to

1373 he was lost to his people, concealed in a mountain fortress where he had been obliged to take refuge. A new king was sought for, a husband for the supposed widow, and Gregory XI offered the crown to Otto of Brunswick. He, however, preferred to marry Johanna of Naples, and Leo emerged from seclusion. But with little better prospects; taken prisoner by the Egyptian sultan in 1375, he was released in 1382, to be thenceforth a wanderer and a pensioner on the Western princes. After his release he made the pilgrimage to Jerusalem, and went thence to Avignon and so to Spain. In Spain he obtained a provision. King John of Castille gave him three lordships, one of them Madrid; and as lord of Madrid King Leo granted a charter to the burghers of the town. But he did not stay in Spain. In 1384 he was in France offering his services as a mediator between Charles VI and Richard II. His offers were not welcome to the English lords, who then held the king in tutelage. They refused him in the first instance his passport—said that though he proffered peace he only wanted money; he was an illusor, and they would have nothing to do with him. Notwithstanding this he not only obtained a safe-conduct but a permit for a cargo of French wine to be brought to England for him; he made an eloquent speech before the king and council at the palace of Westminster; and received a pension of £1000 a year; the first instalment of which was paid into his own hands in gold nobles. He had a passport again in 1392, a few months before his death. His pension was still paid in 1391, in the fifteenth year of the unlucky king: at that time Leo, it was said, had been driven from his dominions; the pension was to be continued until he regained them. Fortunately for the English exchequer, it was not required, for according to the epitaph of King Leo in the Church of the Celestines at Paris, the very noble and very excellent Prince Lyon of Lusignan, fifth Latin king of Armenia, rendered his soul to God Nov. 29, 1393. He left no legitimate issue, and his claims devolved on his cousin of Cyprus. The name of the kingdom of Armenia was thus familiar in

English ears at this time. English sympathy had not flagged during these years. In 1383 another lord de Roos, Thomas, son of the lord who died in 1352, had set out for the East, but died before he left England; his son John fulfilled the vow, and having reached Cyprus, died at Paphos in 1393. A large party of English visitors had appeared there in that year.

James I, the uncle and successor of Peter II, reigned from 1382 to 1398, and was on excellent terms with England. There is a letter addressed by him to Richard II, in July 1393[1], in which he acknowledges the receipt of the epistle of commendation brought by Lord de Roos, and tells him that it was needless, because all the King of England's friends were welcome. He thanks him too for the message which he had received by his most noble cousin, Sir Henry Percy. We learn from this that Hotspur had made Cyprus a part of his great tour; and, as the same year is fixed for the pilgrimage of Henry of Bolingbroke, we may surmise that they came in company. Henry of Bolingbroke, having sailed in July from Lynn, went by way of Prussia, Poland, Hungary, and Venice to Jerusalem; on his return he visited Cyprus, and so back by Italy and Bohemia[2]. King James was a kindly old man, but much tied up between the Venetians and the Genoese. He had accumulated three crowns; he had received that of Jerusalem at Nicosia, as Famagosta was now lost; in 1393 he received that of Armenia, which he handed on to his successors. James had been a hostage or prisoner at Genoa when the Cyprian crown fell to him; he had been sent thither when the perfidious Admiral Fregoso had seized the island; and at Genoa his son, King Janus or John II, was born.

The reign of Janus, thirty-four years long, was one sad struggle, with the Genoese on the one hand and the Turks on the other. The main features of the story are these.

---

[1] Raine, Extracts from Northern Registers, p. 425.
[2] Capgrave, Illustrious Henries, p. 100.

King Janus, with a very natural ambition, stimulated moreover by hereditary and personal enmity, made it the first object to recover Famagosta from Genoa, and for this end, in the year 1402, prepared a force and fleet to besiege the Genoese there. The days of Genoese greatness were over. In 1396 the Doge Adorno had submitted to Charles VI of France, and Genoa had become a French dependency. Famagosta had been won by the Fregosi, the opposite faction to that of Adorno, but the French were, as usual, ready to maintain their claim to conquests under whatever regime they were acquired. On the alarm of war in Cyprus, they sent Marshal Boucicault with a small fleet into the Levant. King Janus prepared for resistance, but the Grand-Master of Rhodes, Philebert of Naillac, interposed as mediator, and a collision was avoided; the poor king had to pay 150,000 ducats for the expenses of the expedition. Peace was however made, and both parties turned their arms against the Mahometan neighbours. The Genoese ravaged the Syrian coast; King Janus plundered the shore of Egypt. Booty was abundant, but the inexorable vengeance of the Sultans was aroused; the ravaging of Syria ended in the loss of the last fragments of Armenian sovereignty; and the plundering of Egypt drew down the Mameluke Sultan on Cyprus. Truces and treaties were made, but were kept on neither side. In the midst of war Cyprus was again, for the third time since the Black Death, devastated by the plague; and the Sultan saw his opportunity; in 1417 he took and wrecked Limasol. In 1420 he swore the entire destruction of the Cypriots, and prepared for a final conquest. Four years after, during which King Janus, although he continued his policy of piratic expeditions, had made scarcely any preparation for defence, he attacked the island, including Cypriots and Genoese in a common purpose of extirpation. Famagosta was taken and pillaged. Two years later the king was defeated and taken prisoner, and Nicosia was sacked. The king's imprisonment lasted fifteen months; during which an attempt was made by an Italian, Sforza Pallavicino, to seize the government. In this he was defeated by the Queen Charlotte of Bourbon, who sent against him Carion of Ibelin, one of the last, if not the last of that great house, of whom anything historical is recorded. Ransomed at an enormous cost, Janus returned in 1427, but thoroughly broken in spirit and despairing of the fortunes of his house. One of his last acts was to marry his daughter Anne to Lewis of Savoy, a connexion which in the next generation helped to place the nominal crowns of Cyprus, Armenia and Jerusalem, among the honours of that aspiring house. He died in 1432, and with him the last sunset gleams of Cypriot glory vanished.

The native historians date the beginning of the downfall to the murder of King Peter in 1369; and if that date be taken we must allow that Petrarch, who thought that that event determined the loss of the East, was gifted with somewhat of prophetic spirit. But I think that, unfortunate as that event was for the Lusignan house, the doom of the Levantine principalities was already sealed. The great plague had swept off the old acclimatised Franks, especially those nobles who, like the lords of Ibelin, had increased and multiplied in the land. With all their faults these nobles were *bona fide* Crusaders; men who, like the first champions, were ready to cast in their lot in a Promised Land, and not, like the later adventurers, anxious merely to get all they could out of it, to make their fortunes. They were swept away. Then there was the antagonism of Genoa and Venice, a piece of history which, so long as history is read in books written in direct hostility to Venice, will be read two ways. Genoa had from the very early Crusades been the ally of France, as Pisa had been the ally of England. Venice had succeeded to the political connexions of Pisa; the tower of the English at Acre abutted on the ward of the Venetians and the Hospitallers; not that during these ages the English national power was of any weight in the Mediterranean, but a good deal of national piety and knight-errantry found expression in pilgrimages which now were conducted by way of Venice, in alliance with the Teutonic knights and the Hospitallers. The final acquisition of Cyprus by Venice, and the extremely unfair way in which it was acquired, seem to have afforded the grounds for supposing that the republic had long coveted the island, and that her policy had been for several generations directed to that end. This crooked policy is contrasted by the hostile writers with the open violence of the Genoese exemplified in the war of 1374, and the seizure of Famagosta. But I confess that I see little to choose between the two, and that what little there is seems in favour of Venice. Neither republic looked at the defence of Christendom as the great thing to be sought. The trading interest, or territorial ambition complicated with trading interest, was the main thing. If Venice profited most by the common policy, it is not so much a proof of previous diplomacy as a result of her longer tenure of power. That the Venetians however had an equal share with the Genoese in weakening the Frank kingdom it is impossible to prove : the Genoese hold on Famagosta was a fatal if not a mortal wound.

But still more powerful agencies were at work. The hands of Christendom were paralysed, and the barbarians were gaining strength and unity. The close of the fourteenth century, an exceptional but a very critical era, seems to show us all nations, all royalties, churches, religions, civilised and barbarous, in a cauldron or a whirlpool from which there was very small chance of emerging whole. A madman on the throne of France, an impotent drunkard claiming the crown of the Cæsars, a frantic absolutist overthrowing the constitution of England ; the see of S. Peter divided between two, three, four Popes ; the Emperor of Constantinople begging money openly in the courts of the West ; the three barbarian powers pitted against each other— providentially, we may say, for who could have resisted their united force—the Ottoman sultan the prisoner of Tamerlane ; the Mameluke sultan only sustained in independence by the contest between the Turks and the Tartars. Yet Europe does emerge; the battle of Nicopolis puts an end to the Crusades; the retreat of the Tartars enables the Ottomans to recover their ground; Byzantium has a respite of half a century, and Egypt of more than a hundred years of Mameluke tyranny. It takes a century more to constitute the great national factors of modern history. But out of the whirlpool little states like Cyprus do not emerge; and after the death of King Janus, the causes that were at work worked quickly and steadily. The immediate cause of the break-up was connected with the same sort of religious disputes which, after occupying half the century in councils and debates, left the Byzantine empire defenceless before the Ottomans. King John III, who succeeded in 1432, took for his second wife, in 1435, Helena, the daughter of the despot of the Peloponnese, Theodore Paleologus. The house of Lusignan had been hitherto, as a matter of necessity, devotedly Catholic; the house of Paleologus was devotedly orthodox; Cyprus was a Catholic kingdom with an orthodox population; a Latin king with a Greek people; the Latin Church was rich, and the Greek Church was not poor, but the political power was engrossed by the former. Helena would not see this. She determined, if she could, to make Cyprus orthodox; she, through her husband, who was a weak and vicious man, refused the papal nominee to the archbishopric of Nicosia, imprisoned him, and was accused of poisoning him. The grand-master of Rhodes came in, as usual, in the part of a peace-maker, and prevailed on the king to receive the prelate; and soon after, in 1458, both Helena and her husband died. But the quarrel had shaken the tottering kingdom; the grand Caraman, the Turcoman ruler of Caramania, took the opportunity of these quarrels to seize Corycus, the last Frank stronghold of Armenia. The Cilician and Syrian begs with the Egyptian sultan formed a league for the conquest of Cyprus, which was foiled by the Rhodian galleys, or the Latin kingdom would have succumbed before the capture of Constantinople. The end was clearly coming, and it was not now a question between Venetians and Genoese, but between Christian and

Moslem, which should take the island as a derelict. The royal house was nearly extinct. Charlotte of Lusignan, the only legitimate child of John III, succeeded him in 1458. She was the widow of John of Portugal, prince of Antioch, who had been poisoned by the creatures of Helena in 1457. She married, in 1459, her cousin Lewis count of Geneva, of the house of Savoy, who was crowned the same year. Her bastard brother, James, archbishop-elect of Nicosia, the son of a Greek lady, whose nose Queen Helena had bit off, was disappointed of the succession, and turned traitor. He aspired to the vainglory of sovereignty, and, having done homage to the sultan of Egypt, invaded Cyprus. For four years Queen Charlotte was besieged at Cherin; in 1464 she fled to Rhodes, and thence to Italy, where, in 1485, she made over her rights and the three crowns she wore to the house of Savoy. James II, a prince of some power, governed or commanded in Cyprus from 1464 to 1473, and to some extent justified his usurpation by taking Famagosta from the Genoese, but his reign was one long series of conspiracies. He was assassinated two years after his marriage with Caterina Cornaro (in 1471), who bore a son after her husband's death. This was King James III, who died when he was two years old. The Venetians held that the rights of the infant king devolved on his mother, and in her name governed Cyprus.

On the details of the Venetian title I cannot now enter; the whole history has been accepted on the evidence of the enemies of the republic, whose story is briefly this. In order to qualify Caterina for a foreign marriage she was declared the adopted daughter of S. Mark, and her husband the son-in-law of the republic. The republic, anxious for the succession, poisoned the son-in-law, who in his will entailed the crown on his children, posthumous and illegitimate, with remainder to the house of Lusignan. But this was set aside by the connivance of Caterina with the Venetians, who, after they had ruled Cyprus for fifteen years in her name, obtained from her a renunciation of her rights in favour of the republic; this was done in 1489; and then,

formally as well as actually, Cyprus became a Venetian dependency, tributary to the Sultan of Egypt. Caterina herself retired
to the Venetian territory, where she lived at the villa Paradiso in
the Trevisan mountains, painted by Titian and patronising the
scholars of the renaissance, until the year of her death, 1510.
After eighty-one years spent under Venice, Cyprus was conquered by the Turks in 1570. From the date then of Caterina's
surrender, and indeed from the death of King James, the history
of the island falls into the mass of that wonderful Venetian
history of which we read so little, but which must contain so
many lessons, and so many warnings for a nation like our own.

The titles of the several royalties which thus came to an
end were claimed as titles easily may be claimed by other
competitors: the Dukes of Savoy called themselves Kings of
Cyprus and Jerusalem from the date of Queen Charlotte's
settlement; the Kings of Naples had called themselves Kings
of Jerusalem since the transfer of the rights of Mary of Antioch,
in 1277, to Charles of Anjou; and the title has run on to the
present day in the houses of Spain and Austria, the Dukes of
Lorraine and the successive dynasties of Naples. The kingdom
of Armenia must, I think, have been dropped; but the Savoyard
claim to Cyprus was held as an offence to the Venetian republic, a point of ceremonial which, in the seventeenth century,
put a stop for thirty years to any diplomatic intercourse between
Venice and Savoy. The successors of Richard I never put in
a claim to the reversion; the quartering of the arms of Cyprus,
which is said to appear on the tomb of Queen Elizabeth, being
no doubt a part of the bearings derived from her great-grand-
mother, Jacquetta of Luxemburg, whose daughter, Elizabeth
Wydville, carried the blood of the house of Brienne and the
Dukes of Athens into the line of York[1]. The Kings of Sardinia

---

[1] The descent is a long one, and there is a question whether the arms are those of
Cyprus at all. But certain claims to represent the elder house of Lusignan had come
into the family of Luxemburg. Jacquetta was daughter of the Count Peter of S. Pol,
whose mother, Marguerite of Enghien, carried the representation of the Counts of

continued to strike money as Kings of Cyprus and Jerusalem, until they became Kings of Italy. There is no recognised King of Cyprus now, but there are two or three Kings of Jerusalem; and the Cypriot title is claimed, I believe, by some obscure branch of the house of Lusignan, under the will of King James II.

So much for the archæology of the question. The interest of England in the affairs of the Levant did not come to an end with the surrender of Cyprus to Venice; for the Knights of Rhodes maintained the defence of Christendom for half a century longer, and England was a close friend of the order until Henry VIII confiscated its estates. The Turcopolier of the Knights Hospitallers was always an Englishman; he was the commander of the light infantry of the order. I have found no list of the Turcopoliers; but in the fifteenth century we have the names of Peter Holt, Thomas Launcleve, or Langcliffe, Hugh Middleton, and John Kendall; all of them would seem North-countrymen. In the last century a medal of John Kendal was found in Knaresborough Forest, and it would seem that he was a member of the family which was particularly marked by its devotion to S. Wilfrid of Ripon. The last known brother of the Order of S. Thomas of Acre, Richard of Tickhill, must also have been a Yorkshire man. The Cypriot king also had a Turcopolier, who, in 1357, was an Englishman. But these are trifles.

I said in my first lecture that I should draw no moral or

Brienne to the Luxemburgs. Mary, daughter of Hugh I, of Cyprus, and his queen, married Walter IV, of Brienne, father of Hugh, and grandfather of Walter V, duke of Athens; Walter V had a daughter Isabel, who married Walter IV, of Enghien, father of Lewis, Count of Brienne and Conversano, and grandfather of Margaret, who was the heiress of Enghien. She married John of Luxemburg, and was mother of Peter, Count of S. Pol. As a claim to the throne of Cyprus, this descent was worthless; but it was a royal descent, and, after the extinction of the Lusignans and the house of Antioch-Lusignan, might be thought to have a value of its own. Queen Elizabeth, however, was in no sense the heiress of S. Pol, much less of Lusignan.

political lesson from the history of Cyprus and Armenia. No lesson can safely be drawn from it, if by lesson we mean absolute instruction or warning that it would be foolish to despise. But it does suggest some generalisations and prompt some questions. We can see that the loss of the Levantine states in the middle ages, that is, the cessation of the defence of Christendom against Mahometanism, was mainly caused by the jealousies of the Christian powers themselves : the determination of the Venetians and the Genoese to set their respective commercial profits above all other considerations. Whilst the Teutonic knights were fighting in the North and the Rhodians in the South, Cyprus, the storehouse of Palestine, was left a prey to the evils out of which the Genoese and Venetians could make their market. It was so in the age that followed : the alliance between Francis I and Solyman paralysed all action by which Charles V and Ferdinand I would have defended the provinces on the Danube and Transylvania, and suffered the Turkish dominion to grow almost unimpeded, until the world began to think that the Turks had a vested interest in the lands they devastated. But the questions which arise are not easily stated, and not easily answered. How can the East be redeemed by the acclimatisation of Northern races ? are the Northern races the only races that can redeem the East, and if so, how are they to be saved from the evils, moral, intellectual, and political, which acclimatisation seems invariably to bring with it ? Are the Eastern races to be redeemed at all, or is that part of the aspiration of the Christian Church and of social philanthropists to be a vain dream ? Is the task of empires to conquer or to colonise ; the task of colonies to extirpate or to develope ? Is a commercial or a military policy the surest agent of civilisation ? Can a worn-out nation be revived and refreshed and recruited by a bracing treatment ? can it be revived at all ? Does the difference between European and Asiatic history consist in the vitality of the historic nations in Europe and the inexhaustibleness of the hive in Asia ? If not, how is Europe to treat Asia, so that the march of civilisation may affect the lands in which the stream of history seems to have long been stayed? if it is so, how shall the East be rescued from the successive waves of barbarism which may be now impending, and how kept alive when those successive impulses are exhausted? Small as our subject was, it was a part of that which touches all, the world's government and the long patience of Providence. "And I said, it is mine own infirmity, but I will remember the years of the right hand of the Most Highest."